READING AND WRITING

READING

AND WRITING

ROBERTSON DAVIES

UNIVERSITY OF UTAH PRESS
SALT LAKE CITY

Special edition published 1993 by University of Utah Press

LIBRARY OF CONGRESS CATALOGING-IN-PUBLICATION DATA

Davies, Robertson, 1913–
    Reading and writing/Robertson Davies.
        p.   cm.
    Originally published: University of Utah Press, 1992.
    (Tanner lectures on human values; vol. 13)
      ISBN 0-87480-426-4
      1. Davies, Robertson, 1913–   — Authorship.
    2. Authors and readers. 3. Books and reading.
    4. Authorship. I. Title.
    PR9199.3.D3Z47   1993
    813'.54 — dc20   92-40787
                                      CIP

Reading and Writing is composed in Intertype Goudy, with decorative embellishments from border slides and matrices, cast in hot metal by Donald M. Henriksen. Printed on acid-free paper.

READING AND WRITING

⫷ READING ⫸

There was a day when, if I were asked to give a lecture, I would search for some recondite subject on which I would be able to amaze my hearers and add to my reputation as a man of wide and various knowledge. But as time passes I find that either my hearers are growing wiser or I am growing stupider, and the likelihood that I can astonish them becomes more and more remote. So when I was asked to give the Tanner Lectures I decided that my best plan was to talk about things that everybody knows and attempt to stir up some discussion which would give the really clever ones a chance to show their strength. That is why my lectures bear the simple titles "Reading" and "Writing."

Every one of you, I am sure, reads and writes, and some of you do so professionally. That means, in our time, simply that you are paid to do it, and not that you are necessarily greatly gifted at those pursuits. Professionalism as applied to reading and writing is a subject on which I shall have some rather severe things to say, because I think the word *professional* is misleading and exerts a bad influence. I shall tell you why later. At the moment we must talk a little more of the actual words *reading* and *writing* and perhaps agree about what they mean.

Most people on this continent can read and write in some degree, though the number of those who cannot is disgracefully large. An astonishing number of those who can read and write think that they do so rather well. I spent twenty years as a journalist, and I met all kinds of men and women who prided themselves on what they called their "communication skills"; they would tell you, with an unconvincing show of modesty, that they thought they could write "a pretty good letter." It was my duty as an editor to deal with their pretty good letters, and I never ceased to be astonished at how badly people expressed themselves who did well in the world as lawyers, doctors, engineers, and the like. When they were angry they seemed unable to focus their anger; they roared like lions, and like lions they roared on no identifiable note. When they wished to express grief they fell into cliché and trivialized their sincere feeling by the awful prose in which they expressed it. When they were soliciting money for charity, they pranced and cavorted in coy prose, or else they tried to make the reader's flesh creep with tales of horrors that may have been true but did not sound true. I used to wonder what made them write as they did, and whenever I was able to find out I discovered that it was because of the dreadful prose they read and the way they read it. They admired cheap stuff, they imitated cheap stuff, and they appeared to have no understanding of how they cheapened their own minds and their powers of expression by doing so.

Do not suppose, however, that I intend to urge a diet of classics on anybody. I have seen such diets at work. I have known people who have actually read all, or almost all, the guaranteed Hundred Best Books. God save us from reading nothing but the best. But God deliver us from contenting ourselves with a steady diet of mediocrity, for it is mediocrity, rather than downright trash, that influences the majority of readers.

Very often nowadays we hear and read the pitiful wails of those who are convinced that reading is in deep decline. They blame television and the movies for this state of affairs. I wonder very often how they square their conviction that nobody reads with the evidence of bookshops everywhere and the proliferation of paperback books which, if not cheap, are at least cheaper than the hardback originals. Most people must be reading or so many books would not be published every year, and it is possible today to be very well read without ever buying a book in hard covers. The literary community, too, seems to be growing at an astounding pace. Wonderful young new writers are hailed every week by eager reviewers. You can hardly throw a stone in the street without hitting somebody who has written a book. People are ready to lay down money in quite substantial sums to listen to authors read, even though most writers are wretched readers. Has there ever been a time when the writer was such a cult-figure as he is today? Every time a writer brings out a book his publishers pay to ship him all over the continent so that people may gaze at him, and marvel at him, and ask for his autograph. Every time a young writer produces something, older writers like myself are entreated to write some words expressive of their awe and delight at the effulgence of his genius. The papers carry news of the large sums that authors are paid as advance fees, sometimes even before they have put pen to paper.

Ah, but there I go, exposing myself as a creature from a bygone age. These new writers do not *put pen to paper* — they put forefinger to word processor, the new device which is supposed to take so much of the pain out of authorship. I do not myself use a word processor, because I am what it is now the fashion to call a technomoron. I have no skill with machines. I fear them, and because I cannot help attributing human qualities to them, I suspect that they hate me and will kill me if they can. However, I am here not to expose my ineptitude but to talk about reading. What I have been suggesting is that there is more reading today than ever before in the history of the world, and that most of it is of no importance whatever.

We all have to read far too much. Every day the mails bring us handsful of material, of which some part must be read, or skimmed. If we are in business, or in the academic world, we have to read essays and documents relating to our work. It is unheard of now for a government body to bring out a report that does not run to a thousand pages; nobody can read it all, but many people must read some of it. We have to read countless letters, often simply in order that we may throw them away. We are deluged with stuff that must be read, and to meet the needs of busy people, procedures of speed-reading have been developed which enable anybody who has mastered the trick to grab the contents out of a mass of print without reading it seriously. Very often all the speed-reader gets out of his speed-reading is the intent of the material read: he does not assess its value, nor does he base his opinion of what is said on the way the case is argued. Indeed, he cannot be said to have *read*, except in the most superficial sense.

It is unfortunate that this craze for rapid reading has infected the universities, where, if anywhere, careful and considered reading and rereading ought to be the rule. Departments of English provide their students with Reading Lists which explain what writers and what works will be dealt with in particular courses. It is understood between the students and the faculty that nobody is expected to read all the books on the list; students are asked only to "acquaint" themselves with what is on the list, so they finish their year's work with a once-over-lightly acquaintance with a staggering array of masterpieces. I do not complain of this procedure: I do not even think it of doubtful honesty. I have seen it at work over many years, and it is a fact that students emerge at the end of the year somewhat less illiterate than they were when they went in. Can one reasonably ask for anything better? But has it anything to do with reading?

Of course it can be argued that reading too much is just as pernicious as reading too little. I recall from my undergraduate days a girl who used to moan, when she was slightly drunk: "I've read everything on the Senior English course lists, and where has it got me?" What she meant was that her reading had not provided her with beauty, or charm, or sexual irresistibility. That girl had gobbled eight plays of Shakespeare, a play by Ben Jonson, all of *Pamela*, the whole eight volumes of *Clarissa*, eight novels by Dickens, one by Thackeray, one by Trollope, a large wodge of Henry James, a substantial vegetarian mass of Bernard Shaw and God knows what else, and at the end of it all her mind was as flat as Holland. All she had gained were thick glasses and a bad breath, doubtless the result of literary constipation. I once asked her if she had read Browning's *The Ring and the Book*, which was an enthusiasm of my own. She had not. She said it was "not required reading," and that was that. But T. S. Eliot was required reading, and she had read him to the bone, without any discernible effect. She did not even get a First Class in her finals. She was the most over-read girl I have ever known, but she still said, "Between you and I." God deliver me from all such.

To speak only for myself, I read a great deal of varied material, including several newspapers. Perhaps because I come of a journalist family, I have never scorned newspapers as many people do. I have long been mindful of the words of Henrik Ibsen, who, when he was asked what he read, replied that he read only the Bible and the daily papers, and there he found everything he needed. And indeed, if you read the newspaper perceptively, you will find the great themes of the Bible, of Homer, of Shakespeare, repeated again and again. When I was a teacher I used to tell my students that if they thought the plot of *Othello* far-fetched, they had only to read the *Toronto Globe and Mail* any Monday morning to find that the plot had been recreated and reenacted in some suburb over the weekend. It is from newspapers that I collect such information as I have about the supposed present crisis in education. By no means all that is said looks backward to some imaginary time when the world was filled with keen and perceptive readers. I have a clipping of a letter to the *Times* of London, in which the writer declares:

> Your correspondent of October 15, 1990, bemoans the influence of television, and says it is the task of teachers to teach children to become readers. Surely the task of teachers is to make children more effective and critical users of information from all sources, of which television is one of the most important. I am a book lover; I have acquired many hundreds and written a few. But the day of the printed book which has been our staple source of information for 500 years, is now passing. Education must look forward, not back.

It sounds eminently reasonable, does it not? It has that calm, no-nonsense ring which impresses speed-readers. But I think the writer is wrong on several counts. I cannot believe that the day of the printed book is passing. A book is such a convenient object; you can carry it anywhere. You can go backward in it, and reconsider something that it said yesterday or last week. You cannot do that with television. The book can present abstract ideas, which television cannot; unless you can take a picture of something, it has no news value for television. Finally, I do not agree that education must look forward at all times; real education looks backward, and gives you a sense of the past against which to measure the present and forecast the future. Television is a good educational tool, but it has its marked limitations. The convenience of the book, as I have described it, will ensure a long life for it, unless we bring up a race that has forgotten how to read.

There are people who declare that we are doing precisely that. A revealing test was made, several months ago, by an international body which estimated the literacy — in which was included mathematical literacy — of twenty-four of the most advanced countries on earth. Unhappily, your nation [the United States] came twenty-fourth on the list. Do not think I am exulting; my country ranked twenty-third. The young people of this continent were found wanting in every important skill — and you will remember that mathematical skills were included. They read badly —

which is to say that they could not intelligently relate the content of a paragraph of prose — and they could not express themselves in writing in simple, unambiguous, grammatical sentences. In your country this has caused an understandable uproar, and subsequent investigation has revealed that nearly a million children in the United States graduate from high school every year unable to read at the level expected of eleven-year-olds. Enlightened employers are spending heavily on remedial classes for secondary-school graduates. Think of that — the bosses now have to educate the workers because the schools have failed to do so. The New York Telephone Company recently rejected several thousand applicants for a handful of low-level clerical jobs because none could summarize a simple paragraph. When your Scholastic Aptitude Test authorities attempted recently to impress the school authorities with the importance of reading and writing, and attempted to introduce one — only one — compulsory essay as a test of analytical and communicative ability, radical educators, politicians, and other lobby groups protested that such a test discriminated against black and Hispanic Americans and recent immigrants. To put it bluntly, the inabilities of the disadvantaged minorities were to establish the standard for the nation.

So what is to be done? Is all lost? Not at all, but the salvation lies not with the government bodies but with individuals — with hundreds and thousands of men and women who decide that this diseased concept of democracy shall not prevail. Whenever I talk in this way — and I have been doing so for more than thirty years — somebody is sure to protest that I am proposing the establishment and recruitment of an intellectual elite. My reply is enthusiastic agreement: that is precisely what I am doing. What is an elite? Is it not a body which values the best above that which is less good? Your country has never hesitated to let it be known that it leads the world in certain respects. You do not insist that your national standard of living should be that of your humblest citizens. You do not inhibit scientific research lest some less fortunate country should feel left out and protest that your scientists are elitist. Your moral standards as expressed by your politicians are the wonder of less ethically grandiose folk; I have always thought your invincible morality was a heritage from the Pilgrim Fathers, who were so unremittingly moral that the Old World couldn't stand them for another minute and kicked them out. You do not conceal the fact that you are the wonder of the world. But in matters of intellect you are strangely unwilling to assert yourselves. Although many of the world's leading intellectuals are citizens of the United States, you do not, as a nation, take pride in the pleasures of the intellect, enjoyed for their own sake, as adjuncts of the truly good, well-rounded life.

I wish you would give it a try. But let me say at once that I am not calling for some great national movement, with a president and several vice-presidents, and innumerable committees, and of course a vast drive for funds, and fortnightly meetings, and prizes for those who recruit the most members, and special prices for the old and the crippled — excuse me, I mean the disadvantaged. Anything of that sort would be wholly against the kind of gentle but insistent change in the national life that I most earnestly wish to see. What I call for is a multitude of revolutionary cells, each composed of one intelligent human being and one book of substantial worth, getting down to the immensely serious business of personal exploration through personal pleasure. Your nation was born of revolution. Don't I know it! My Canadian forebears were Loyalists, who lost in that war and had to make a run for it to a new country. Why not another and equally decisive American Revolution — a revolution of the intellect? Why are we on this continent so afraid of using our brains?

Am I preaching to the converted? I wish I thought so, but you will excuse me if I have my reservations. I have known far too many university graduates, in this country and in my own, who, as soon as they have received the diploma which declares them to be of Certified Intelligence, put their brains in cold storage and never use them again until they are hauled away to the mortuary. What, you will say, do you speak thus of our doctors, our lawyers, our — God bless us all — our graduates in business administration? Yes, I do. Surely we all know scores of professional men and women who, apart from their professional con-

cerns, seem not to have enough brains to butter a bis-
cuit. They probably had intelligence once. But when
their university had given them its blessing, they
thought that enough had been done for one lifetime.

Anybody who cares about the matter knows that
the intellect requires constant attention and renewal.
The notion that someone who has graduated from a
university has thereby been victualed for a long voyage
through life as an intelligent human creature, is totally
contradicted by common observation. And when I
speak of intellect, you must not suppose that I mean
merely that really rather humble ratiocinative ability—
that power to reason about the ordinary concerns of
life and to reach conclusions from given facts. I do
not even mean that same ratiocinative faculty carried
to a higher level, where it attacks complex, but still
wholly finite problems. I use "intellect" to include
all that vast realm of thinking and feeling that goes
beyond the merely puzzle-solving work of the mind
and establishes, so to speak, the very fabric and atmo-
sphere in which life is lived and from which it is per-
ceived. And when I talk of education I have no desire
to belittle the powers of reason, but only to assert the
power of *feeling*, the power of *sympathy* in the true
meaning of that word, which enlarges our understand-
ing of every aspect of our lives. We are quick to say
that it is man's power of abstract thought that sepa-
rates him from the animal world, but how rarely do
we say that it is man's power to *feel* through a broader
spectrum of emotion and sympathy that also makes

him human — and, because human, capable of conduct that ranges from the godlike to the villainous.

There are many ways of educating our feelings, but I recommend reading as that which is most ready to hand. We can all do it. But *do* we do it?

I beg you to pardon me if I seem to stress the obvious in what I am saying. I do so because it is so obvious that it is often overlooked or undervalued. I do not suppose there are many present here who would dispute my statement that literature is an art, and that as an art it is able to enlarge and refine our understanding of life. But do we treat it as an art? Consider the care we take when we listen to music. Do we attempt to do so in a room full of people who are talking, and who interrupt us frequently for opinions? Do we increase the speed of the hi-fi in order that we may get through a symphony in time to rush away and do something else? Do we stop a recording partway through a movement because we have to fulfil some demand of ordinary life, then start the machine up the next day at the same place, to finish what the composer was saying? Do we skip here and there on the record or tape, looking for tunes that appeal to us, or rejecting passages of exposition that we find dull? No, of course we do none of these absurd things and would condemn anybody who did do them as a barbarian who had no feeling for music. Why? Because we regard music as an art, and our civilization demands that serious and sometimes almost religious attention be paid to it.

Literature, however, is something quite other. It is the drudge, the unconsidered odd-job man of the arts. Who among us can say that when he reads he does not rush, and skip, does not stop in improbable places, does not indeed commit the literary sin against the Holy Ghost, which is to gobble a book in order to be able to say that he has read it, without having given the book a fair chance to declare to him why it should have been read?

I have already agreed that much of the reading we have to do is unworthy of anything beyond superficial attention, but when we take up a book that is a work of art, or is so intended by the author, should we not treat it better? The worst offenders in this realm are book reviewers. I know, because I have been a reviewer myself, and I have been ashamed of the superficiality with which I read books in order that I might be able, within a certain fixed time, to deliver some sort of opinion about them. One's opinion about a book should surely rise slowly from the impression that the whole book has made, perhaps a considerable time after it has been read. Of course that cannot be the way a reviewer works, but certainly we should bear this fact in mind when we read reviews, which are written often in great haste, to establish the reputation of the reviewer, rather than to give a careful assessment of what an author has worked very hard to make as good as he can.

Now I am going to talk about the way in which I think a book *should* be read, and if what I say seems unbearably simpleminded I ask you to hear me to the end. First of all I think it is desirable to put aside some time for reading — perhaps an evening, or an hour, or half an hour, or even fifteen minutes, but a time in which to read and do nothing else and pay no attention to anything but the book.

We can read any way we please. When I was a boy, and was known to be fond of reading, many patronizing adults assured me that there was nothing I liked better than to "curl up with a book." I despised them. I have never curled. My physique is not formed for it. It is a matter of legend that Abraham Lincoln read lying on his stomach in front of the fire; you should try that in order to understand the extraordinary indifference to physical comfort that Lincoln possessed. I have read about children who "creep away into the attic" to read, and Victorian children's stories are full of children who cannot read anywhere except in a deeply embrasured window seat. You have to find your own best place for reading, and for most of us in the Western world it is sitting on a chair with a decent light — though for Lincolnians, of course, firelight is the thing. I have forgotten those people of whom it is said that they "always have their noses in a book." This makes reading difficult, but as I have said, you must suit yourself.

You then read your book, somewhat more slowly than modern educationists recommend. Remember, you are trying to find out what the book has to say. You are not straining to reach the end, in order that you may read something else. If you don't like the book, you do not have to read it. Put it aside and read something you do like, because there is no reason at all why you should read what bores you during your serious reading time. You have to read enough boring stuff in the ordinary way of life, without extending the borders of ennui. But if you do like the book, if it engages you seriously, do not rush at it. Read it at the pace at which you can pronounce and hear every word in your own head. Read eloquently.

I know this is heresy. People who teach reading are dead against what they call "verbalizing." If you verbalize, you lose time. What time are they talking about? Time is one of the great hobgoblins of our day. There is really no time except the single, fleeting moment that slips by us like water, and to talk about losing time, or saving time, is often a very dubious argument. When you are reading you cannot save time, but you can diminish your pleasure by trying to do so. What are you going to do with this time when you have saved it? Have you anything to do more important than reading? You are reading for pleasure, you see, and pleasure is very important. Incidentally your reading may bring you information, or enlightenment, but unless it brings pleasure first you should think carefully about why you are doing it.

Everybody used to verbalize as they read. Indeed during the Middle Ages people read aloud, and everybody knows the story about the scholar who had to discontinue his studies because he had a sore throat. Because they verbalized — I hate that word, but I can't find another — they truly took in — drank in, one might almost say — what they read and it was impressed on their minds forever.

Verbalizing is also one of the best critical procedures. If you meet with a passage in a book that seems to you to be, in some way, dubious or false, try reading it aloud, and your doubts will be settled. The trick of argument, or the falsity of emphasis will declare itself to your ear, when it seemed to be deceiving your eye. Lots of young people come to me to ask my advice about writing. I haven't much to give them, and if they think anyone but themselves can teach them to write, they are sadly mistaken. I am fond of a story about Beethoven, who was approached by a young man who asked him how to become a composer. "I cannot tell you," said Beethoven; "I really don't know." "But you have become a composer yourself," protested the young man. "Yes, but I never had to ask," was the answer. I tell the young people who come to me to try reading their work aloud, to see how it sounds. "Oh, but I'm not writing for performance," they say. "Oh yes, you are," I reply, and often they are mystified. But in truth writing *is* for performance. The great works of imagination — the masterworks of poetry, drama, and fiction — are simply indications for performance which you hold in your hand, and like musical scores they call for skilled performance *by you*, the artist and the reader. Literature is an art, and reading is also an art, and unless you recognize and develop your qualities as an interpretative artist you are not getting the best from your reading. You do not play a Bach concerto for the solo cello on a musical saw, and you should not read a play of Shakespeare in the voice of an auctioneer selling tobacco.

This business of verbalizing, of reading so that you hear what is read with the inner ear, is an invaluable critical method when you are reading poetry. Much of what passes as poetry is perishable stuff. Not long ago I was making a comparison between the *Oxford Book of English Poetry* as it appeared in 1900, edited by the late Sir Arthur Quiller-Couch, and the latest edition, edited by Dame Helen Gardner. It was an astonishing revelation of change in taste — in the taste of scholars of great reputation who as critics command respect. But I permitted myself — critical worm that I am in comparison with these godlike figures — to wonder if Sir Arthur and Dame Helen had taken the trouble to read aloud all that they offered to the world, with justifiable confidence in their authority, as a survey of the best verse of five centuries. Had Sir Arthur ever really tested "A garden is a lovesome thing, God wot," on his tongue?[1] If he had done so, could he have missed that what he took for honey was saccharin? Perhaps so; there are elements in literary taste that seem not to be things of reason but of some-

---

[1] Thomas Edward Brown, "My Garden."

thing relating to time, which determines taste. When Dame Helen includes

Lay your sleeping head, my love
Human on my faithless arm[2]

most of her readers will applaud, but what will readers say in another seventy years? Modern disillusion is unlikely to last forever, and nothing rings so hollow as the angst of yesteryear.

Reading to hear, rather than merely to comprehend, explains much about the poetry of earlier days. Old ballads, which seem somewhat simpleminded, with their bleak stories and their repeated refrains, when they pass over the eye, leap into vivid life when they are heard, because they belong to a tradition of poetry which had not renounced the delights of rhyme, rhythm, and the quality of incantation which our distant forebears valued in poetry. Poetry which has decided to do without music, to divorce itself from song, has thrown away much of its reason for being, and a recognition of the element of music in poetry narrows the gap between, for instance, Keats and Byron, which might appear to a reader who had never *heard* them to be almost unbridgeable. Until quite recently there was an academic fashion for looking down on Tennyson, who was said to be mellifluous but simpleminded. But *listen* to Tennyson, and his music will tell you something that the closest sort of mute analysis can-

[2] Wystan Hugh Auden, "Lullaby."

not do, and his stature as a poet is restored and per-
haps increased thereby.

I have been talking about poetry, and I do urge
you to renew your acquaintance with it, if by chance
you have not been reading much poetry lately. Perhaps
this is the point at which I should advise you, if you
are reading for pleasure, to read several books at once,
and to keep on your table a book of poetry, as well as a
novel, some essays, and perhaps a play or two. The
notion that you have to read solemnly through one
book before you can allow yourself to take up another
is simple Puritanism, probably left over from child-
hood. If you choose to be an epicurean reader, which
is what I am recommending, there will be times when
nothing but poetry will satisfy your appetite, and you
must have poetry readily at hand. Pehaps you like to
keep up with what the young poets are doing, and that
is admirable, but I urge you also to read some poetry
that has been tested by time, and which does things
that the moderns do not seek to do, or perhaps — I
say this almost apologetically — cannot do. One of
the things I miss in modern poetry is joy, exuberance,
sheer delight in life. That is a quality that preserves
a poet marvelously.

> Ty hye, ty hye! O sweet delight!
> He tickles this age that can
> Call Tullia's ape a marmosite
> And Leda's goose a swan.

Who writes charming invitations to pleasure in a kind
of splendid giggling frolic spirit like that nowadays?

Not the people who write lyrics — if they may so be
called — for rock music; their joy seems to have its
roots in disarray of the mind. But the little squib that
I have just quoted springs from joy that is unalloyed,
and it was written in a time when the plague and war
and the ill-will of nations were just as prevalent on the
earth as they are today, and the average expectation of
life was about thirty-two years.

I myself have a taste for Browning. There are times
when nothing but Browning will do. He is not par-
ticularly musical, and that is odd, because he is one of
the few poets who was a technically trained and skilled
musician. His language is knotty and there are times
when his reader feels like

> The old man of Ashokan
> Who loved to chew wood, mostly oaken;
>> Very often he'd quip
>> With a smile on his lip,
> Ah sho' can gnash oak in Ashokan.[3]

Browning's tough colloquialism used to be held against
him, and as an undergraduate I encountered profes-
sors who would quote:

> Irks care the crop-full bird?
> Frets doubt the maw-crammed beast?[4]

— and then go off into paroxysms of dusty academic
mirth at what they thought was Browning's willful

[3] Morris Bishop.
[4] Robert Browning, "Rabbi ben Ezra."

clumsiness. But once you have accustomed yourself to his voice, Browning has golden things to say, and I have been a lifelong champion of *The Ring and the Book*, which is neglected by many readers because it is long and intimidating. But it is also a very great poem, and you do not have to read it all at once. But to sense its worth you should read in it, and reread, at various times in your life. Frequently it recalls to me the Loathly Damsel of medieval legend, who was repellent at first encounter but who, when embraced, changed into a girl of inexhaustible charm, wisdom, and beauty.

What I have just said about rereading is a point I should like to stress. The great sin, as I have said, is to assume that something that has been read once has been read forever. As a very simple example I mention Thackeray's *Vanity Fair*. People are expected to read it during their university years. But you are mistaken if you think you read Thackeray's book then; you read a lesser book of your own. It should be read again when you are thirty-six, which is the age of Thackeray when he wrote it. It should be read for a third time when you are fifty-six, sixty-six, seventy-six, in order to see how Thackeray's irony stands up to your own experience of life. Perhaps you will not read every page in these later years, but you really should take another look at a great book, in order to find out how great it is, or how great it has remained, to you. You see, Thackeray was an artist, and artists deserve this kind of careful consideration. We must not gobble their work, like chocolates, or olives, or anchovies, and think we know it forever. *Nobody ever reads the same book twice.*

Of course everybody knows that, but how many people act upon it? One of the great achievements of literature in our century is Proust's *A la recherche du temps perdu*; in the edition I have it runs to twelve convenient volumes. In my experience people tend to read it when young, and never to look at it again. But it is not a young person's book. Of course young people should read it, but they should go on reading it or reading in it during the life that follows. When I read it as a young man, the homosexual exploits of the Baron de Charlus seemed extraordinary dispatches from an unknown world; nowadays, when one can meet a mini-Charlus every day of the week, the extraordinary quality has gone. But what has not gone— what is indeed freshly understood — is Proust's serious and compassionate treatment of this theme in a book of many themes. Charlus is one of those great characters whom we know better than we know most of our contemporaries, and his creator's attitude toward him and his tenderness toward the Baron's dreadful disintegration enlarge our own sensibility, and give us a different attitude toward excitable protests on behalf of "gays" — as for some reason they are called, in our own very different, un-Proustian society. The Baron would have shrunk from being typified as "gay."

So it is also with another towering creation of this century, James Joyce's *Ulysses*. One cannot, of course,

measure what Molly Bloom's magnificent soliloquy at
the end of that book has done to enlarge and reshape
our ideas about women, but one knows that its in-
fluence has been vast. When Sigmund Freud asked his
supposedly unanswerable question—"What do women
really want?" — he had not read what Molly wanted
or he would have phrased it differently. It is not that
she *says* what she wants, but she makes us *feel* what
she wants, and it is something far beyond the range of
any sociological or psychoanalytical answer. Molly
wants to live on a mythological level, and that cer-
tainly does not mean that she wants to posture as a
goddess or indulge in any pseudoclassical antics; it
means that she wants a largeness of perception, a wider
dimension of life, a psychological freedom that the
modern world does not give her. She wants a rich
simplicity. And that is the whole thrust of the book.
Unaware of the fact, Leopold Bloom and Stephen
Dedalus are living out a great classical theme in their
dingy Dublin lives, and the greatness of what they are
doing eludes them. Eludes them not because they are
stupid — they are nothing of the sort — but because
it is part of our fate never to see our destiny as a whole
or discern the archetypal forces that shape our lives.
Molly does not see these things either, but she has an
intuitive sense of them, and thus she is able to long for
them when the men, corseted in reason and logic, can-
not draw so near to this aspect of truth.

Ulysses is a wonder, and we can recur to it time
and again with the certainty of finding new pleasures

and new insights. It is also one of the funniest books in our language. The fun lies not in obvious jokes; it is in the grain of the prose, and it rises from the extraordinary mind of the author. When we read, we must always be aware of the mind that lies behind the book. Not that we may be wholly persuaded by it, or that we should have no minds of our own, but that we may share it and be shown new meanings by it. Also that we should assess it. When I was a professor I seemed to meet a great many students who were wholly possessed and beglamoured by Oscar Wilde, and some of them were, for a few weeks, mini-Wildes, dealing extensively in *réchauffé* wit of the 1890s. Sometimes I suggested that they examine, not the refulgent surface, the shot-silk elegance of his prose, but whatever they were able to discern behind it of the mind that had created such beautiful things. It is a Fabergé mind, and although we should not like to be without Fabergé, we should not wish to make him our standard of artistic achievement. There are people who insist that Wilde ranks with Congreve as a great writer of comedy. Consider both minds: Congreve was wise — worldly wise as well — in a degree that Wilde never achieved, kindly, good, generous, fatuous man that he was.

Joyce is an Irishman of a different stripe, and Wilde's admirers might describe him as a dirty-fingernails writer. If Joyce's fingernails are dirty, it is because he has no objection to grubbing in the dirt, if the dirt has anything to tell him. And he has taught us one of the lessons of our century, which is that the dirt has very important things to tell us, because it is from the dirt that we all spring, and no disease is so fatal to an adequate understanding of life as overre-finement, which is inevitably false refinement. For refinement of feeling is surely a quality we bring to everything we touch, and not something which cuts us off from a great part of human experience. Modern hygiene has banished much of the physical dirt of an earlier day, but the lessons that are hidden in the dirt must not be forgotten.

Of Joyce's other remarkable book, *Finnegans Wake*, I shall not speak, because I have not yet come to any conclusions about it. I know few people who have read it, and of those, I meet fewer still who appear to me to have come anywhere near to under-standing it. I grope in it, holding a candle that is plainly marked "Manufactured by C. G. Jung and Co., Zurich." It is not a candle that Joyce would have approved — he hated Jung because Jung told him something he didn't want to hear — but the Jungian candle is the only one I have.

I hope you do not think that I am being trivial, or treating you with less than proper respect, because I am talking so much about novels. When I was an undergraduate there were still academics who thought novel reading an inferior sort of literary enjoyment. But a good novel has its roots in life as surely as a good poem and usually more truly than the work of most essayists. It was when I was young that I read the opinion of a critic — popular at that time and now almost forgotten — John Middleton Murry, that "A truly great novel is a tale to the simple, a parable to the wise, and a direct revelation of reality to a man who has made it part of his being." I have never forgotten that, and I test the novels I read by its acid, seeking for gold, for gold plate, and for dissembling brass.

The simplest function of the novel is the tale, but only someone who has never tried it thinks that the discovery and relation of a tale is simple work. The wish to be told a story never dies in the human heart, and great storytellers enjoy a long life that more subtle writers sometimes envy. Consider the stories of Sherlock Holmes. Unless you are beglamoured by them, they are queer reading. The mysteries that confront the great detective are tailor-made for his style of detection; they are puzzles suited to a particular puzzle solver. Confront Holmes with a simple back-street murder or theft, and he would probably have to confess his inferiority to the Scotland Yard bunglers he despised. But the tale-telling is so skillful, the contrast between Holmes and Watson so brilliant, the upper-middle-class level of crime which is all that Holmes will touch (you observe that he has no truck or trade with the likes of Jack the Ripper) is all so deftly handled by Arthur Conan Doyle that he has created a legend that seems to be increasing sixty years after the death of its creator. Will Virginia Woolf last so long? It seems to me that I see the mists closing in as her novels give place to scandalous revelations about her life.

Then comes the parable. What is a parable? A moral tale, is it not? Such novels are very popular because, whatever appears on the surface, our time loves a display of moralism; innumerable novels are rooted in the words of Saint Paul: "Be not deceived; God is not mocked; for whatsoever a man soweth, that shall he also reap." That is the message of Tom Wolfe's hugely popular best-seller *Bonfire of the Vanities.* What is its message? It seems to be couched in modern, rather grotty language: keep your nose clean; don't risk everything for the big bucks; never trust a dame. But behind this street wisdom is the wisdom of Paul, served up with the pepper and tabasco that persuades so many innocent readers that they are geeting something undreamed of in the past.

Now, what about the book which is a direct revelation of reality? We all have our favorites, and they are the books that accord with the reality life has brought to us. We cannot hope to grasp total, all-embracing reality. For many people these are the great blockbusters — novels like *War and Peace, Crime and Punishment, The Magic Mountain, Middlemarch, Remembrance of Things Past.* I have known people who found this sort of revelation in *Don Quixote,* which I can understand but not accept as my own; I have known others who found it in *Tristram Shandy,* which I confess puzzles me. One must find one's own great novels, which seem to illuminate and explain portions of one's own experience, just as one must find the poetry that speaks most intimately to oneself. For one reader it is Shakespeare's *Sonnets*, for another Wordsworth's *Prelude*, for another *The Ring and the Book*. And so it would be possible to go on elaborating and extending lists, because the choice is great and individual preference the final factor in making a choice. And in addition to these milestones on the most traveled roads, the real enthusiast for reading will find byways, like the works of Rabelais, or Burton's *Anatomy of Melancholy*, or the magpie accumulations of John Aubrey. It is absurd to speak of these books as byways, but I do so because I do not meet many people who read in them frequently, or indeed at all.

How dull he is being, you may think, as I draw near to my conclusion. How like a Professor. He is simply parroting Matthew Arnold, with his tedious adjuration that "Culture is the acquainting ourselves with the best that has been known and said in the world, and thus with the history of the human spirit." But I assure you that I mean no such thing, and I have always had my reservations about Matthew Arnold, who was too cultured for his own good; he seems never to have listened to the voices which must, surely, have spoken to him in dreams or in moments when he was off his guard — voices that spoke of the human longing for what is ordinary, what is commonplace, vulgar, possibly obscene or smutty. Our grandparents used to say that we must eat a peck of dirt before we die, and they were right. And you must read a lot of rubbish before you die, as well, because an exclusive diet of masterpieces will give you spiritual dyspepsia. How can you know that a mountain peak is glorious if you have never scrambled through a dirty valley? How do you know that your gourmet meal is perfect in its kind if you have never eaten a roadside hot dog? If you want to know what a masterpiece *The Pilgrim's Progress* is, read *Bonfire of the Vanities*, and if you have any taste — which of course may not be the case — you will quickly find out. So I advise you, as well as reading great books that I have been talking about, read some current books and some periodicals. They will help you to take the measure of the age in which you live.

I hope you are not disappointed in the advice I have been giving. Certainly I have not flogged you on to feats of endurance and intellectual stress. Quite the contrary, I have urged you to relax, to read more slowly, to reread books that speak to you with special intimacy, to act out your fictions in your minds, as if you were a great theatrical director with infinite choice in casting, in decor, in all the adjuncts that produce a convincing atmosphere. I have urged you to allow your poetry to sing to you so that you may hear the authentic bardic voice wherever it is to be found. This is reading for pleasure, not to become immensely widely read, not to become an expert on anything, but to have read deeply and to have invited a few great masterpieces into your life. Again, I suggest that you should read deeply, rather than widely.

Many years ago — it was in 1960, in fact — a book of mine was published by the late Alfred Knopf, called

A Voice from the Attic; it bore that curious title be-
cause one of our Canadian poets had described Can-
ada as "one and none, pin and pine, snow and slow,
America's attic," and I was speaking from that attic.
When it was published in England it bore the less
provocative but probably more descriptive title *The
Personal Art* — and that personal art was reading.
Its first chapter was titled *A Call to the Clerisy*, and
it said rather the sort of thing I have been saying in
this lecture. It proposed that an educated class should
recognize itself in North America, and take into its
own hands the literary influence which had been
pretty much abandoned to the universities and the
academic critics. By an educated class I certainly did
not mean people of substantial means with university
degrees; I meant anybody who knew how to use a
public library and did so with zeal and devotion. I
expressed no enmity toward the academic critics but
I did say that I thought their professionalism and the
need they had to establish personal reputations made
them less-than-perfect guides for the public at large.
I called for the rise and self-recognition of a group of
readers whom I defined as "those who read for plea-
sure, but not for idleness; who read for pastime but
not to kill time; who love books but do not live by
books." And to that group, the members of which
are to be found everywhere, I applied the almost for-
gotten word *clerisy*. It is not so aspiring as *intelli-
gentsia*, which is a word that frightens many people.
I once had a friend who was applying for a position in

a large financial house — a rather senior position —
and when he was being interviewed by the Big Boss,
the Big Boss said, rather truculently: "Do you con-
sider yourself a member of the intelligentsia?" "No,"
replied my friend, "a member of the intelligentsia is
what I aspire some day to be." I need hardly tell you
that he did not get the job. Rich people are usually
afraid of an intelligentsia, because intelligentsias have
so often been used as stalking-horses for revolution-
aries. But *clerisy* is a mild term, one might almost say
a Trollopian term. It could not frighten the most neu-
rotic banker. And the clerisy do not want to take any-
thing from anybody; they merely want to recover what
was their own in those distant days before so much of
our intellectual life was abandoned to the universities.
They want to have a say in the world of books. They
want the world of books, through them, to have its
influence in the national life — social and political. To
return, somewhat apologetically, to Matthew Arnold,
they want the history of the human spirit to have its
influence in the history of our own times.

✒ WRITING ✒

In the first lecture I talked of reading and now the theme is writing, but of course you understand that the two are inseparable for the purposes of such a discussion as this. With respect to reading, I am only one voice among millions, but in matters of writing I may claim to be one among thousands, for, though it sometimes seems that everybody in the world wants to write, comparatively few really do so in any serious sense.

Like every author who has achieved even a modest measure of success, I get bagsful of letters from aspiring writers who ask me questions that make it plain that they are unlikely to do anything very much in that art — for it is an art when it is practiced creatively, and by that I mean in the writing of poetry or drama or fiction, and in a slightly lesser degree in the writing of philosophy, history, and essays. As you see, I exclude criticism, for although some critics do write admirably in the technical sense, I cannot persuade myself that their work is creative. If they wish to disagree with me — and as a usual thing they do — that is their privilege.

The people who want to be writers are often seekers after a formula, or even a magic spell, which they are hopeful will bring them to their heart's desire. For they are very serious — serious, that is to say, in their desire to be known as writers, though they are often reluctant, or unaware, in everything that is involved in the actual work of writing. They think that a writer is a romantic creature, widely admired and amply rewarded. So they write to me — and to thousands of other writers, I am certain — asking, "How did you become a writer?"

If I have time I give them an answer, because I take them seriously and think that if they are sufficiently determined to write to me it is common courtesy to reply. But my answer is unlikely to give them comfort, because I tell them that I never became a writer: I was born a writer. My family, even beyond the confines of my parents and my brothers, were writers, by which I mean that they were journalists ranging from simple reporters to writers of political comment, essays, reviews, and editorial opinion. Consequently I grew up supposing that everybody wrote; wrote to order, to length, and to time, and received payment for it. I think I must have been at least twelve years old before I became aware that not everyone writes and that indeed many people find it a task of daunting complexity and difficulty. But I was bred to the trade, and at school, and later, I was a great enterer of contests where money prizes were offered for essays. "That's *my* money," I thought, without any particular vanity; I knew I could get it, I delivered the goods, and I got it.

Apart from this confidence, I had other advantages. My parents were strict grammarians, and my brothers and I learned the English language by ear, which is not wholly a good way to learn, because I still have trouble identifying grammatical structures by name, though I know them as matters of usage. Any publisher's reader can throw me into confusion by asking technical questions. Not only were my parents grammarians, they were demon pronouncers and enunciators, and often there was a dictionary on the family table, to be a guide in pronunciation and usage, and I well remember the scene of Homeric mirth and derision when my older brother pronounced "truculent" as if the first syllable were "truce."

I think this was a good way to bring up a boy to be a writer. Acrobats start their children on the high wire as soon as they can walk, and a writer ought to begin before he has graduated to solid food. But as you will see, not everybody has my good fortune, and I can hardly offer the people who write to me Mrs. Poyser's advice: "You must be born again and born different." [5]

I know several writers, and they did not begin as I did. They became writers because that was their destiny, I suppose.

---

[5] George Eliot, *Adam Bede*.

If somebody is truly a writer, he will find it out and he will understand that if there is any romance attached to the vocation, it is balanced by a number of unromantic circumstances, for the biographies of writers make it clear what a tough and enduring breed they are. There have been writers who have burst upon the world, to its astonishment and delight, but most writers have to establish a reputation over a period of time. That is where the toughness comes in; early discouragement is the rule, and much work is done before important lessons are learned.

Speaking for myself, my great wish was to be a playwright because the theater was, and still is, the chief pleasure of my life. But I wrote seventeen plays before I found that I was not to be a playwright, because my conception of comedy was not to the popular taste. I was thirty-eight before I turned to fiction and fared rather better, though I swear I was writing my novels from the same source, and in the same vein, as I had written my plays. So I became a novelist and an essayist.

Another question that my letter writers often ask is, "When do you write?" To which the only honest answer is that I write when I can. For the greater part of my life, the luxury of devoting the best hours of the day to my writing has been denied me. I have no one to blame but myself. I have always had a job. For twenty-one years I was a journalist, and for much of that time the editor of a daily newspaper. I was then invited to join the faculty of the University of Toronto as — this is ironical for a failed playwright — a specialist in English drama. I was also appointed as the head of a college for graduate students. Thus for forty years I had a full-time job, and I wrote usually at night, when the day's work was done.

I do not in the least regret it. To begin with, my job meant that I was able to pay my own way as a writer. I have never received a grant to enable me to write, and I value that freedom very highly. I could not square it with my conscience to take money to enable me to do something that I was not sure I could do — and I swear to you that I have never set to work on a book with complete confidence that I would be able to finish it in a way satisfactory to myself. I have been criticized for my attitude toward grants to writers. I am told that the modern grant-giving bodies are the descendants of the aristocratic patrons of the past. My only reply is that Dr. Samuel Johnson seems to me to have said the final word on those aristocratic patrons, and I do not believe that their modern descendants are really indifferent to what happens to the money they hand out. Nothing — including grants — is for nothing. We hear much high-minded prattle in these days about the writer's freedom, and I think he best asserts his freedom when he refuses to take money from anybody to do what he himself has chosen as his life's work. Robert Graves has said that a poet who writes for money will be rejected by the White Goddess, from whom all true poetic inspiration comes. I think this is true of all serious writing and I do not think Graves's reference to the White Goddess either fanciful or superstitious: she is the only real patron and if you are not content with her patronage she will not care. But in the final summing-up, rather than in the royalty statements and the publisher's returns, it is her patronage that will mark you as an artist or merely a glossy hack.

For academic projects the rules are probably different, but for the creative writer I see no possibility of accepting handouts and maintaining total freedom. Let the writer get a job, and look after himself, and be under no obligation to call anybody "Massa."

There was another reason why I thought my best course was to earn my living as I pursued my work — by no means remunerative for many years — as a writer. It kept me in touch with the world of realities. If you read the lives of writers, you will find that very few of them have been reclusive. Flaubert was so, but not Stendhal or Balzac. Dickens's life was a whirlwind of charitable obligations. Tolstoy ran a large estate. Dostoevsky met the world at the gaming table, and Proust met it in the salons of the aristocracy. Anthony Trollope was a senior civil servant. I will not burden you with a tedious list of examples, because I am sure you know the truth of what I am saying. The worst thing that can happen to a writer is to draw in upon himself and his work until he knows nobody except other writers; he is then reduced to the literary desperation of writing a book about a man who is writing a book, and when he does that we know he is finished. I was always glad of the association with a wide variety of people that my work, first as a journalist and then as an academic, made necessary. I particularly valued the association with people much younger than I that the university made inescapable. It is very bad for a writer to become imprisoned in his own generation.

I have another point to make about the value of doing something in the world other than being a writer. The daily task keeps you from writing too much. You are not obliged to keep bread in your mouth, and in the mouths of your wife and children, by snatching at every occasional article, by attending political jamborees as a "special observer," by patching other people's work together to make a television program, or accepting commissions to write things for big corporations that look like books but are in fact a low form of hackwork. Even if you are a successful novelist, it is not in your best interest to have to bring out a book every year in order to please your public and build up an income from paperback sales. I am sure we can all think of writers who write far too much; their talent has become diseased, hypertrophied because of continual gross and indecent solicitation of the imagination. If you reply that Balzac and Dickens did it, I invite you to look at the infinitely larger number of writers who have done so to their hurt.

How the work is actually done is in part an exploration of drudgery, of daily application, of heaping up the pile of finished pages as the beaver builds his dam. But if you are really a writer, you probably like that drudgery better than anything else you could possibly be doing. It is during those hours of drudgery that you are most in touch with what is of greatest value in yourself. You are creating something, and therefore you are to some extent an artist; you are doing it by means of the technique you have painstakingly acquired, and perhaps mastered, and therefore you are a craftsman, and there is a special delight in plying one's craft.

Again I recur to the questions I am asked by the people who write to me. Young people — schoolboys and girls who are put up to this kind of pestering by their teachers — often ask, with youthful bluntness, "Where do you get your ideas from?" My usual, perfectly honest reply is, "I don't get them; they get me." If you have to rummage around finding something to write about, perhaps your vocation is less insistent than you suppose. Often these young inquirers read a book of mine — read it once, in the desperate rush which is apparently inseparable from modern education — and then they tell me what it means. Or rather they inquire about what it means indirectly, by a form of words that fills me with the desire to kill them. They look me in the eye and declare, "What you're trying to say is . . . ," and that is where I choke them off, roaring, "I'm not *trying* to say anything; I *am* saying it

with all the art and skill that I have acquired in a life-
time of hard work." But what I really ought to say is,
"The book does not call for your reductive, half-baked
explanation; it exists, and to you it may be a tale or a
parable, or a direct revelation of reality; you will gain
nothing by pulling it to pieces. It is like a clock, and
if you observe it understandingly it will tell you what
time it is in my life and yours, but if you pull it apart
you will have nothing but a handful of junk." I do not
often go so far as to say this, because I know that these
children are being taught a system of criticism which
is only criticism of a low order, and which is really an
escape from direct experience of a work of art. I do
not wholly blame the teachers; they are confronted
with classes of students whose understanding is of the
uttermost variability, and to talk about art to such a
chance assembly is to embark on stormy and danger-
ous seas. The teacher's job is to teach, and artistic
sensibility is not to be taught, so it must be feigned.
I must say in justice that from time to time I encounter
students who really do know what a book is and ap-
proach it as a work of art, and receive from it what-
ever a work of art is able to give them at a time when
they are still green in understanding.

About adult critics I shall not speak. They rank
from sensitive and deeply intelligent writers whose
opinions must be respected, even if they are not shared,
on down the steep descent to the large group whom
Yeats dismissed as "sciolists and opinionated bitches."
Every time a writer publishes a book he must run the

gauntlet of criticism, the worst of which comes from—
again I quote Yeats —

> A leveling, rancorous, rational sort of mind
> That never looked out of the eye of a saint
> Or out of a drunkard's eye.[6]

I am speaking to you very personally. Whenever
I meet with harsh or scornful criticism — and I assure
you that I do, with each new book, encounter some
of this—I reflect that my first novel came out in 1951,
and it was dismissed by a majority of critics as an
amusing but inconsiderable piece of work; but it is still
in print, and sells pretty well, and some very intelli-
gent people write to me who have found it much to
their liking; whereas the criticism is forgotten and
many of the critics are dead and rotten. The best
advice I know for the writer on the matter of criticism
was given by Thornton Wilder; he said that a writer
should certainly read criticism of his work and give
it adequate but not prolonged consideration, or else he
would find that the critic had wormed into his mind
and was writing his next book. To which I would add
that it must always be remembered that the critic is
seeking to enhance his own reputation, and may not
be wholly scrupulous about the way he does it.

When reading reviews, it is necessary to consider
the way in which they are written. If a critic can really
write, it is probably worthy of your attention. But

[6] William Butler Yeats, "The Seven Sages."

many critics are miserable craftsmen in the art they seek to guide.

Perhaps it is too much to expect the author to distinguish at all times between serious criticism and newspaper and magazine reviewing. The latter is likely to be hasty, and undertaken by someone under stress and perhaps burdened by a sense of his own peripheral relationship to literature. But there — is one to regard anything that is published as "literature"? How much of what appears every year must be dismissed as honest in intention, but trivial in attainment?

To return to the aspiring writers of whom I spoke a few minutes ago, and who eagerly seek guidance about how to become writers, where are they to look? Not far, for there are all kinds of books that profess to teach methods of writing, fiction and non-fiction, poetry and the steamiest sort of prose. I bought one such magazine when I was thinking about what I would say to you. From time to time I receive through the mail offers to teach me to write, by some infallible method, but I have never had time to accept them. But in preparation for today I thought I had better find out what these helpful people were offering. The cover of my magazine proclaimed "How to Write Passionate Love Scenes . . . and Still Respect Your Typewriter in the Morning." Much is suggested in that title. Is the reader to expect that he will not only learn to write passionate love scenes, but that he will himself experience them vicariously? To a certain sort of mind, the prospect is alluring. The imaginative preparation, or foreplay; the turning down of the sheets, so to speak; the actual writing, or deliciously prolonged orgasm; the sense of achievement, of having transformed erotic fantasy into art. And you can do it over and over again, without fatigue or disgust —

> ... thus, thus, keeping endless holiday
> Let us together closely lie, and kiss,
>   There is no labour, nor no shame in this;
> This hath pleased, doth please, and long will
>   please; never
> Can this decay, but is beginning ever.[7]

I was astonished when I read the article to find it quite sensible; its counsel was, "Don't overdo things." But the title, as it appeared on the cover — that was aimed straight at the eager, desirous heart.

The magazine was full of advice, which may be good. I don't know because little of it concerned me. I don't particularly want to know "how to write irresistible nonfiction" nor do I want advice about computers because I do not own one and could not manage it if I did. I don't worry about collecting from slow-paying magazines. I don't want to know how to improve my writers' group, because I shrink from the notion of writers' groups; I don't want to master the building block of poetry and don't believe such a thing exists; nor do I seek "a playful guide to being a Southern writer." I was grateful that at Christmas nobody

---

[7] Ben Jonson's translation of Petronius Arbiter's poem which begins "Foeda est in coitu et brevis voluptas."

WRITING

gave me the foolishly suggestive "Take an Author to Bed" poster. I am interested that the magazine calls loudly for novels in which "safe sex is eroticised and characters are sensuously — and routinely — conscious of their own and their partners' health" because this shows that the magazine really has its heart in the right place and wishes to be associated with a "caring community." Literary aid against AIDS, in fact.

As a writer, I have my share of intuition, and as I looked through that magazine I had a strong sense of the sort of reader at whom it was aimed: a lonely person, whose youth was slipping away; a reader who will hopefully cut out the coupon that is appended to an advertisement that begins, "You Can Make Up to $9,800 in 24 Hours!" and which describes the literary life as "The Royal Road to Riches"; a reader unsophisticated enough to believe that writers live marvelous social lives, eat and drink very high on the hog, and have access to unlimited, apocalyptic sex. A wistful reader and, I fear, an untalented one.

It is very sad. People of that sort do not, so far as I know, imagine that they could learn to write music by mastering a few easy tips, or that they could paint pictures that anybody would want. What on earth makes them think that they can be writers? It would be interesting to talk about that.

I should be sorry if you received the impression from anything I have said that I regard writing as being wholly remote from the ordinary concerns of life, and unheeding of what is going on in the world.

The world around the writer presses upon him as it does on everybody else, and alters his way of working, although I do not think it alters what he most seriously works with, and has worked with ever since the printed book became generally available.

Ever since 1945 we have heard a great deal about the writer who is said to be *engagé*, meaning involved in current affairs and politics and social movements. The idea is one which many people, including some good writers, have found attractive. It seems to get the writer out of his solitary cell and into the forum. He devotes his skills of persuasion to manifestly good causes — or causes which seem good at the time — and politicians and demagogues and leaders of all kinds like to see a few writers on their side; it suggests an intellectuality which may not otherwise be strongly apparent. Unquestionably some writers are deeply moved by political and social causes, and they write with power to support whatever they think is necessary to bring about a better world. Every revolution has had a few writers involved in it at the beginning; by the end they are frequently either disillusioned or dead. But it would be wrong to dispute their sincerity or their goodness of heart.

There are many more writers, however, who regard themselves as *engagé* because it gives them a direction they would not otherwise have. It is a truism to say that a writer writes best when he writes of something that presses deeply upon his consciousness, and demands to be heard. It is from the depths that the real inspiration rises. But there are scores of writers, sufficiently successful to attract attention from a public which knows their names if not their works, and upon whom nothing really presses very strongly. They want a theme; they want something that gives direction to their work. They are looking for a cause, and a vast array of causes lies open to them, waiting for them to make a choice.

They write books about all sorts of things — the wretchedness of the drug addict, the hard lot of the black people, the Spanish population, the native people, the misery of the woman who needs an abortion, or hasn't had one, or has had one and wishes she hadn't, the problems of the woman who has to make her way in a man's world where, literally, every man's hand is against her; indeed the misfortune of womanhood is almost unlimited in its profusion of themes. They espouse causes of every sort, and they are especially indignant about groups which, for one reason or another, are victims of discrimination. They are very severe upon The Rich, who are so wanting in compassion for the misery which gives rise—or seems to these writers to give rise — to their wealth and privilege. The world of such writers as these is filled with mute, inglorious Miltons, to whom they are eager to lend a voice.

Do not suppose for an instant that I am jeering at any of these themes, all of which have their validity as the understructure of fiction. But I am — well, not jeering, but certainly questioning the quality of the writing which emerges when a writer seizes upon a theme because it is for some reason popular, rather than because he has any strong initial feeling about it. Very often such writers try to make up for this want of depth of inspiration with a mass of research, which they insert into their books with a shoehorn, and which impresses readers who are awed by bundles of facts. When I read about a novel that it has been "extensively researched" I take it as a warning signal.

Unquestionably there are writers who are truly *engagé* and whose writing is powerful and moving. Such a writer, for instance, is Nadine Gordimer, whose novels about affairs in South Africa are justly celebrated. But when you read them you know that they have been deeply felt, rather than merely "researched," and that they are descriptions of life as it is, and studies of individual character, rather than polemics directed against a political regime. To revert to a classical example, it is the deeply felt passages and pathetic characters in *Uncle Tom's Cabin* that convince us, not the abolitionist harangues.

As opposed to the writers whom I have been describing are those who do indeed write about what presses most powerfully and insistently upon them, and it is in the work of such writers that we most frequently encounter that quality of individuality that is called "style." Style is an elusive quality, and one of the amusing things about the world of criticism is to watch critics chasing it, like children trying to put salt on the tail of a robin. They invent categories of writing, and then try to confine writers within these critical jails, talking of "minimalism" and "post-modernism" and "magic realism" and a dozen others, as if these things had real existence and were not simply gases extracted by the critics from works of strong individuality. Of course there are writers — writers modestly gifted but full of industry and aspiration, like the ones who write about politics and social wrongs — who leap from their chairs crying, "By Gum, that's it! I've been a minimalist all these years and didn't know it!"— and henceforth are increasingly minimal (if you will pardon the contradiction in that phrase) until finally they achieve total nullity. A style, or a special quality of writing, is not something that can be pulled on like a shirt. You cannot, so to speak, decide to "join the minimalists." Unless a style rises irresistibly from within the writer, as evidence of his individuality, it is not a style. It is a mannerism, an affectation, and, although it may be amusing for a while, the time will come when the writer finds it is getting in the way of his real talent. I do not say that there are never writers who do indeed find a new or apparently new way of writing. Unquestionably there are, somewhere, a few genuine "minimalists" who may never have thought of themselves in that way until the critics baptized them; but their minimalism is their gift, and other writers imitate it at their peril. For any writer, unless he is a young beginner looking for his own style, to imitate another writer, is to confess a fatal want of talent.

Writers who would never think of imitating any-
one else must, however, give heed to the literary atmo-
sphere in which they work. You cannot write fiction
nowadays in the mode of a century or two centuries
ago, unless you are doing so for well-understood rea-
sons of pastiche. All my life it has been one of my
pleasures to read novels of the early nineteenth cen-
tury. Not, I assure you, only the novels of the masters,
but the second-raters, and even sometimes the third-
raters. They are not half so bad as you might suppose.
They are full of entertainment and they offer wonder-
ful glimpses of past life and past ideas. It takes a sur-
prising amount of talent to be even second-rate, and
Bulwer-Lytton and Harrison Ainsworth and Charles
Lever were very able craftsmen and by no means in-
tellectually trivial. But one of the things I envy them
as I read is the leisure with which they could lay out
their stories. They back into their narrative like a re-
luctant horse being coaxed between the shafts of a
cart. If they are writing about a family (and when
are they not doing so?) they tell you its background
and ancestry in a degree of detail which is quite aston-
ishing. Dickens has parodied this approach marvel-
ously in the first chapter of *Martin Chuzzlewit*. If they
are writing about a battle they do not spare you a de-
tail of what the ground was like, and what the com-
manders made of it. Indeed Tolstoy comes as near to
spoiling *War and Peace* as a genius can come to de-
stroying a masterpiece, by telling us what he would
have done if he had been Napoleon. We forgive these

writers, because we know that they were writing for a public which had apparently immense time for reading novels. Of course they had nothing of the kind; they had precisely as much time as we have today, but they didn't have the movies and television to compete for their leisure. Even Sir Walter Scott — unquestionably a great genius — was prolix to such a degree that I confess to you, in my shameless seniority, that I have never been able to read most of his novels without a great deal of skipping. I don't have to read about his moors and his mountains — I've seen 'em, and all I need is to be told that something is happening on a moor and a mountain to conjure up in an instant what may take him three or four pages of heavy, and to me confusing, prose to describe. When I was a boy my parents and their friends used to go into ecstasies about Hardy's description of Egdon Heath in the first chapter of *The Return of the Native*. But in these days I, and hundreds of thousands of others, have visited Egdon Heath, or have seen some other heath of equal literary weight, and although I value Hardy's art, I would not dream of trying to do myself what he has done, nor would any living writer I can think of. Nor would I wish to maneuver a pair of lovers into the likelihood of a sexual union as gingerly as do the writers of the nineteenth century. Like so much else, sex has speeded up.

The movies and television have made it necessary for modern novelists to get on with the job as fast as they decently can. All those immensely skillful tech-

niques of cutting and montage and general sharpening
of the technique of narration in which film and tele-
vision are so adroit have influenced modern writing.
Henry James, giving advice to writers, cried, "Drama-
tize, dramatize, dramatize!" Give as much actuality as
you can to the scene of your story, but do not linger
over it and make it a primary element in what you are
writing. The visual imagination of the modern reader
is much greater than that of his great-grandparents. It
is said, cynically but with a terrible ring of truth, that
the modern film is made for viewers with the intellect
of a twelve-year-old. Emotionally and intellectually
this may well be true, but the visual imagination of a
twelve-year-old today is acute. If something is hap-
pening in a city street, he does not need the street to be
set before him, garbage can by garbage can. He has
seen all the city streets he needs on the large screen
or the small one.

So it is also with scenes of action. A great novelist,
like Trollope, moves from scene to scene with a de-
liberation that readers would resent in a modern novel.
And writers of lesser quality, like Willkie Collins, who
was thought to write so sensationally that his work
was almost dangerous to young readers, seem almost to
crawl, as their narrative proceeds. The modern novelist,
who has to compete for his readers with the devotees of
the little screen, cannot do anything of the sort. He must
get on with the job, and he can depend on his readers
to be as brisk as he is in developing the narrative.

The narrative — that's the great matter. Not so very long ago writers like E. M. Forster and Virginia Woolf could be dismissive and even contemptuous of mere narrative. And it must be said that their art was sufficient to conceal a serious want in their works, but not all writers can follow where they trod, nor would they wish to do so. Nowadays there must be narrative — a story — because the readers want it, and if the writer has an eye on a possible film or TV version of his book, it is an absolute necessity.

I am often asked by young people, whose idea of success as a writer is involved in the notoriety and the money that come with film and television versions of a novel: "When are they going to make a movie of one of your books?" I have to say that I do not know. Film directors have shown interest in my work, but they always confess to me that they cannot interest the money which goes into making a film in anything so peculiar as the kind of books I write. Where's the hero, for whose role some popular young star could be engaged? Even worse, where's the heroine? I have been told by more than one film director that my most popular novel is impossible for film, because the heroine is described as one of the ugliest women in the world, and where's your star who would put up with that? The stories, they say, are great, but the characters are simply not translatable into film, unless, of course, I permit extensive revision along film lines which are by no means broad in their scope.

Once or twice I have tried to talk to film people about my ugly heroine. I explain to them the extraordinary psychological fascination of the medieval legend of the Loathly Damsel, whose splendor of spirit is confined within a hideous body, and who becomes beautiful only when she is understood and loved. I advise you not to talk to resolutely Hollywood minds about the Loathly Damsel. Their eyes glaze, and their cigars go out, and behind the lenses of their horn-rimmed spectacles I see the dominating symbol of their inner life: it is a dollar sign. The minds of vendors of popular entertainment are set in cement. Their recipe for success is: the Mixture as Before. They sincerely believe that success can be repeated endlessly, and it is against their resistance that any sort of originality or freshness must assert itself.

When Henry James said, "Dramatize, dramatize, dramatize," what, in fact, did he mean? His own works make it clear that he did not call for what used to be called "a rattling good yarn." Simple narrative, though he thoroughly understood it, had no special hold on him. He was too great a master to neglect it, and when one is called upon to do so it is quite possible to say what his books are *about*. The story is clear enough. Something happens. This distinguishes him from many writers who have sought to follow in his steps, who have been so overwhelmed by the rich allusiveness and implication of his style that they cannot see the wood for the trees, and they write books and short stories which are not, under examination, about anything very much; they are stifled by overrefinement, and it is wholly false to imagine that James was overrefined, whatever the intricacies of his expression. Think of his plots, and it is surprising how tough they are; they might have served Ibsen. His decisive action, however, is psychological. So what did he mean by his urgent advice to dramatize?

I think he meant, simply, that the writer must *show* what is happening; he must not describe it coldly, as might a bystander. Things must happen to his characters. Because so much of the action in James is psychological, an obtuse reader or writer — and people of cultivation and extensive education are perfectly capable of being obtuse — might suppose that nothing is going on. But as P. G. Wodehouse — a master of narrative art in quite a different milieu — once said, action in a plot is not simply a matter of the one-eyed Chinaman coming up through the trapdoor and shooting the butler on every page. Thrillers depend on such obvious devices, but great novels are psychological as well as physical in action, and a first-rate novelist must have psychological insight, as well as a story and a style.

To continue for a little longer with narrative, I want to stress my own conviction that it is vital to serious writing. Some writers are impatient with it, and the great example is Shakespeare, who seems not to have cared much about physical plots; and his work abounds with examples where he has seen beyond a perfunctory and almost incredible plot — *Measure for*

Measure gives us an example — to a psychological action that results in a great play. A very simple on-looker could find pleasure in the tale, and doubtless over the centuries many simpleminded onlookers have done so. Narrative preserves a piece of writing as graces of style alone cannot do. The great example is *The Arabian Nights' Entertainments*, in which the sorceress-mistress of the Great Shah continues her narratives so compellingly that she cannot be resisted. The tyrant must permit her to live if he is to hear how the tale ends. There must be something of Scheherazade in any serious writer of novels, and that is what I want to talk about now.

Much of what I wish to say is summed up in a remark of the late Vladimir Nabokov, when he was discussing the writing of André Malraux: "The longer I live the more I become convinced that the only thing that matters in literature is the (more or less irrational) *shamanstvo* of a book, i.e. that the good writer is first of all an enchanter. But one must not let things tumble out of one's sleeve as Malraux does." He was referring to the clichés, imprecisions, and pretentious passages in the work of Malraux, which in Nabokov's opinion almost ruined him as a writer to be taken seriously.

What is *shamanstvo?* Russian friends have translated it for me as "enchanter-quality." Not simply stage magicianship, where one may perhaps allow things to fall out of one's sleeve, like the inept Malraux, but the real quality of the enchanter, the weaver of spells who may, through his spells, reveal unexpected and marvelous things about life, and thus about ourselves.

How does he do it? Is *shamanstvo* something that can be learned, or acquired by hard work? Here I come to a difficulty, because in our democratic age it is thought to be indefensible to suggest that there is anything that is not achievable by anybody. We know it is not so, but we turn our official, our public face against it. We encourage children to think that they can do anything. We praise them as creative, when in fact their drawings and stories are original only in that the children have no technique and have not yet set any bounds to their aspirations; they will learn to do that soon enough. But the fact has to be faced by anybody who seeks to work in any of the arts that there is no substitute for talent. As a musical friend of mine says, "If you haven't got it, you've had it." Art is much older than democracy, and art is uncompromisingly elitist. Devotion to the magazines, like the one of which I have spoken, which promise big money and quick success, will not make you a writer of any substance, and neither will the most stifling immersion in Matthew Arnold's best that has been known and said in the world. Writers of any substance are a special breed of people, and apart from their gift, it is not a breed that is necessarily agreeable or interesting.

If you want to be a writer, and are not one, you may take comfort in the fact that you are not a vulgarian, like Dickens or Balzac, or a bounder like H. G. Wells, or an embezzler like O. Henry, or an

unwashed bully like Samuel Johnson, or a jailbird like
Cervantes and Bunyan, or a pitiful self-deceiver like
Wilde, or a sour invalid like Pope, or a hypocritical
drunk like Addison, or an unlucky gambler like Dos-
toevsky, or a snorting, sneering snob like Nabokov.
You are a delightfully normal, admirable, lovable
human being — you are just not a writer. You may
have a splendidly rational intellect; very few writers
have ever been so endowed though they have some-
times an uncanny gift of seeing through a brick wall.
You may be an accomplished amorist and have a cata-
logue of your conquests like Don Giovanni; few writers
have ever been good at that game. You may be rich;
writers are never rich, even when they have plenty
of money; there is something in their make-up that pre-
vents them from ever feeling really rich. You may be
happy, and a happy writer is virtually unknown, even
among humorists; indeed humorists are often very sad
men. I urge you to rejoice in your luck. If you haven't
got *shamanstvo* you haven't got it, and that's that.

But we need not give up on our search to find out
what *shamanstvo* is.

> Tell me, where is shamanstvo bred
> Or in the heart, or in the head
> How begot, how nourished?
> Reply, reply.

Well, I think we have decided, for the moment at least,
that we do not know how it is begot, but we may
profitably look to see where it is nourished, and we
will begin with language.

It is extraordinary how few people have any real feeling for language, or any sense that it is one of the greatest and most inexhaustible playthings with which our human state has presented us. It is an unhappy truth that education, or partial education, which is all that most of us can claim as our own, seems to be destructive of the sense of language. It is often among simple people that truly effective and poetic expression is heard. I once heard a Welsh countrywoman in a bus talking to a friend about a local politician: "Every word he says is like a scratch from a rusty nail," said she, and I was struck by the novelty and aptness of her words. At the college where I spent twenty years we had a cleaner, a tiny woman of no great strength but mighty spirit, and one day one of our young men, a notable melancholic, said to her, "Nelly, are you happy?" To which she responded with a radiant face, "Happy! I'm so happy sometimes I have to wake up in the night, just to laugh!" Education seems to rid us of this directness with language. But a writer must have it. His language may be spare or it may be profuse, he may lean toward the demotic and the colloquial, or he may like to juggle with torches and sharp swords, but he must have a way of using words that commands attention, not by its singularity necessarily, but by its aptness, or sometimes by its reduction of a complex idea to an astonishing and revealing simplicity.

Language preserves a work of literary art when the ideas it contains have become familiar, or perhaps even unendurable. We delight in the plays of the

Restoration because of their strong, vigorous, and elegant deployment of language, although the society they depict and criticize is very strange and perhaps repellent to us. The plays of Bernard Shaw are perhaps more powerful today than they have ever been, for although the notions they put forward are now old hat, the way in which they are put forward is so delightful, so classically chaste in expression, so unexpectedly funny even after the twentieth hearing, that we cannot be without them. Language in such writing as in these plays is not the drudge of the intellect but the winged horse of poetry, even though the plays appear to be in prose. We must never underrate what Thomas Mann so slyly called "the finer and much less obvious rhythmical laws of prose."

During the past few years a number of writers seem to have sickened of the simplicity of language which used to be considered a mark of quality.

> Prefer the familiar word to the far-fetched.
> Prefer the concrete word to the abstract.
> Prefer the single word to the circumlocution.
> Prefer the short word to the long.
> Prefer the Saxon word to the Romance.

What excellent advice it is, and how it was beaten into my generation of schoolboys. And, of course, with my inheritance, it was dinned into me at home, along with the totally false assurance that if I ate my crusts I would have curly hair. But one may tire of even the best advice, as one may tire of writing according to those precepts. Would we wish to be without the heraldic splendor and torchlight processions that are the sentences of Sir Thomas Browne? Would we wish to sacrifice the orotund, Latinate pronouncements of Samuel Johnson? Would we wish that Dickens had written in the style recommended by the brothers Fowler, who framed the rules I have quoted; what would then have happened to Seth Pecksniff, Wilkins Micawber, and Sairey Gamp, I ask you? The Fowler brothers, God be with them, were writing for the guidance of, most probably, civil servants, and among civil servants *shamanstvo* is an undesirable quality. But a writer who possesses *shamanstvo* will not consent to be bound by such precepts, any more than he will consent to wear shoes that are several sizes too small. He delights in language, and he frisks, rolls, and wallows in it when he feels that way.

You can all think of modern writers who send their readers scampering to the dictionary. Anthony Burgess, Paul Theroux, John Fowles, Samuel Beckett, Kurt Vonnegut, Peter De Vries, and of course Nabokov, who loved to bemuse his readers with a word that he, not born to the language, used with elegance. The great example of course is James Joyce, but there have been few writers except Beckett who have followed in his steps without ungraceful stumbling. Some time ago I was sent a copy of *The Oxter English Dictionary*, which gave examples of unfamiliar words used by modern writers. I was one of them, and I confess that I was surprised that the word *glamour* in its true sense was thought strange; I had always thought it meant enchantment, in either its noun or adjectival form, but apparently many people think differently. The word *lickerish*, which I had always understood to mean "lecherous," is apparently unfamiliar, though in my childhood it was used by children both in its true sense and of that black candy with which we used to threaten our teeth. You never can tell what words will seem strange to your readers, and probably the best course is to pay no attention, and let them find out, if they wish. If they don't wish, perhaps they should confine their reading to the works of Barbara Cartland, who has, at the age of eighty-nine, just sent her latest romantic novel to her publishers. It brings her score up to five hundred books, and not a thing in them to puzzle the pretty head or bring a blush to the cheek of the Young Person.

Language is a part of *shamanstvo*, for you cannot weave a spell without words. But words alone are not enough. A story is not enough. To weave the spell the writer must have within him something perhaps comparable to the silk-spinning and web-casting gift of the spider; he must not only have something to say, some story to tell or some wisdom to impart, but he must have a characteristic way of doing it which entraps and holds still his prey, by which I mean his reader. He must have a way of saying his say which is not that of the civil servant painstakingly explaining the applications of a tax, but which comes to the reader with a special, unmistakable, individual grace.

And where does that come from? My own ideas on that subject may not appeal to all of you, but I am convinced that this special quality is the product of the writer's access to those deeper levels of his mind that the depth-psychologists call the Unconscious. It is not a particular possession of the writer, this Unconscious, but the ability to invite it, to solicit its assistance, to hear what it has to say and impart it in the language that is peculiarly his own, is decidedly his gift and what defines him as an artist. He may not be — very probably is not — fishing up messages from the Unconscious that astonish and strike dumb his readers. It is much more likely that he is telling them things that they recognize as soon as they hear them — you see I am recurring to my earlier insistence that what is read should be heard and not merely apprehended by the eye alone — but which they have not been able to seize and hold and put in language for themselves. I know of no instance of this quality more concentrated or more powerful than the second part of Goethe's *Faust*, where a world of insight and wisdom and spiritual enlargement is given form and when we read it — or better still if we have an opportunity to see it well realized on the the stage — we do not find ourselves in a world unknown and strange, but rather we know that we are in a world that has always existed within us and which for the first time we begin to apprehend.

Of course *Faust* is not the sole example of this refreshing and life-enhancing revelation. We find it in great novels. Dostoevsky said that you do not have to go outside the mind in order to find God and the Devil, and he spoke truly. We find portions or glimpses of this revelation in novels which have been written with *shamanstvo* in some degree. Such books tell us what we have it in us to know, but have not fully seized by our unaided efforts.

Thus the book which may be a tale to the simple reader — and the tale comes first, as I have tried to make plain — or may be a parable to some who like to explain what lies behind the tale, may also be, at its best, a direct revelation of reality which, when it comes, leaves us enlarged and in possession of some new ground in the exploration of ourselves.